You Will Be Just Fine

Finding Newness Through Your Grief

Ify Odugbemi

Dedication

I dedicate this book to everyone who is dealing with grief or in the face of a terrible loss. You might feel shattered and stuck, and it may feel like you're in a season of darkness, but be assured that the morning will come and you will see the light again. Your grief will not kill you, but it will strengthen you. And as you take one day at a time, my prayer is that the Holy Spirit himself will take you by the hand and comfort you and lead you on the journey forward.

. . . and to Anuoluwapo Grace Odugbemi, who is forever in our hearts.

Review

You will be just fine! As stated by the author, this is the message the book carries. Of the many things I appreciate about the book one that stood out for me was how the author draws from her experience, gives us a comprehensive narrative of her experience with grief because of the loss of her daughter, and the likely responses from people who find themselves as a support network to the one grieving. It is a practical book. The author takes us into the world of her once reality; she does not hold back. I believe this book can support anyone going through any kind of experience that speaks loss and is struggling to find their way.

Thanks again for the opportunity.

Loliya Kagher

This book is awesome (this is no hype).

Grief is an aspect of living we as human try as much as possible not to talk about.

The writeup is well-articulated, properly bible-versed, and most importantly, your writing structure and diction made it seem like you are having a Face-to-Face conversation with the reader.

I'm extremely impressed.

I'm very sorry for the late delivery; I was unintentionally carried away by the book. I read over 20 pages not even remembering I was supposed to change the errors (I lost an elder brother who was my closest pal in the family) because I felt the book was just talking to me.

Ivy Editor

ACKNOWLEDGMENT

I want to thank:

My Dada & Father in Love. Prof Timothy Obi & Eng. Temitayo Odugbemi

My Mama & Mummy in Love. Mrs Sylvia Obi & Mrs Simisola Odugbemi

My Pastors- Dad & Mum Gbenle for holding our hands through it all. You are priceless.

All my brothers and sisters.- Chika, Oby , Nkem, Emeka, Sola Rotimi, Funmi, Abi, Winston

My best friend & Hubby fondly called Honey- Dami Odugbemi.

My Book Coach – Florence Igboyaka (Fondly called Chinny)

My Special Sister –Tosin- Iyawo Ogaga- Thanks for Helping with the Editing of the book. I appreciate you big.

Loliya Kagher for reviewing this book.

My home church, Fountain of Love RCCG Aberdeen- you are a great support network even in stormy times.

I also want to thank EVERYONE who ever said anything positive to me, or encouraged me, fed me, prayed for me.

My Special sisters – Dupy Omotosho(You are rare), Oyin Adekoya, Mope Lammond, Laide Akinsomi, Uchechi Opara, Tobi Kasali(Hugs),Ugochi Okorie, Henrietta Okonkwo

(Mother), Imoh Ejumotan, Chichi Ofor, Glory Elofuke (My Personal Doc), Deola Dada, Wunmi Williams, Juliet Akinsanmi, Felicia Amalu for consistently being there through my Journey to Recovery. Mrs Abe , thank you.

Ejiro Sanya- You are special.

I want to thank God above all because without God; I wouldn't be ……… Period.

Table Of Contents

FOREWORD

"...Weeping may endure for a night, but joy cometh in the morning."

Psalms 30:5b

In this Scripture, while we are so focused on the joy promised ahead, we often ignore the reality that there may be times of weeping too and this is not because we are the 'chiefest of sinners'

As children of God, we have the joy of the Lord as our Source of strength and inspiration, but as humans, there are unpleasant seasons we go through, and not too many people know how to manage their seasons of grief, anger, frustration, loneliness, and pain.

Remember, the Lord never promised us a trial-free journey through life, but He did promise His presence when we go through the fire and overwhelming waters - our seasons of hurt and pain.

(Isaiah 43:2)

We do not have a High Priest who is not touched by the feelings of our infirmities; Hebrews 4:15

Jesus wept at Lazarus' tomb. He identified with them in their time of pain, and restored their joy again.

Are you grieving over the loss of a loved one? Are you depressed? Are you hurting? In this life-changing book, Ify encourages us to find solace and relief in the Arms of the Comforter. It is not the end. Stop reliving your moments of sadness daily. There is still life after a loss.

It is my prayer that this book guides you, not only on how to "move on", but on how to "move forward" and find joy again.

Thank you Ify for giving this book as a powerful tool in life's journey. The Lord shall give it great wings to soar to the Nations of the Earth

Funke Felix-Adejumo

PREFACE

As a lot of people know, grief is an exceedingly difficult thing to deal with, especially when it leads to depression and great uncertainty about the future. For most of us, it is an extremely tough task to handle things like disappointment, depression, distress, frustration, and bereavement.

Because of the experiences I have been through, I realise how important knowledge is when it comes to handling grief. I know there are many books, seminars and teachings out there about this topic, and in their rights, they have helped countless numbers of people overcome difficult times. My decision to write this book did not come from a place of joining the bandwagon but to share from a personal place, my experience and understanding of dealing with grief with respect to my background and the Christian context with which I found myself.

As I thought through all that life has thrown at me up to this point, I realised that my understanding of grief and grieving found their expression in my responses and the responses of others as I went through my moments of pain and healing, and this is what I have decided to share in this book.

From my experience, I talk about the definition of grief and how we can clearly understand the grieving process by exposing the different stages of grief and understanding what God's heart is for us in such times. The process of healing is a long and tedious one, and as you walk with me on my own journey, I trust that the Holy Spirit will walk with you through yours as He leads you to the people you can rely on in such difficult times.

Sometimes, we experience Grief upon Grief when we are exposed while in our initial grief to those who do not know how to handle our fragile state. We might be offended in the process, but we must understand the place of forgiveness in our healing process.

Through this journey, we will also learn how to reach out to others in their dark times with the light of God's healing love as we remain in the posture of worship, knowing that no matter what, God is good.

I am incredibly grateful that I have been given such a privilege to share with the world, something that only a few years ago, I could never speak out loud. I thank you for kindly coming on this journey with me, and I pray it will be a rewarding one for your heart and soul.

Chapter 1:

My Story

It is imperative to me that people understand the importance of having God as a source of strength and a guiding force when touched by grief. Unfortunately, no one is immune to grief. This is because in life we are faced with the reality of losing loved ones or other things that have grown attachments in our hearts, like a job, a pet, our home or source of livelihood. We experience grief even in times when our health fails, or we are robbed of investments that have taken years to grow. We face the most horrible forms of adversity even as Christians, but it is our cry for help to God and the acknowledgement of our need of His mercy that leads us out of our challenging times.

I prayed to the LORD, and he answered me; he freed me from all my fears. Psalm 34:4 (NLT)[1]

Most mothers would agree with me that losing a child, whether young or old, is not something they would ever want to go through. As a Christian, and as many of us do, I pray every day that God keeps my loved ones safe. I pray that my children will grow up and live long and prosperous lives as impactful members of their society.

---

[1] New Living Translation or bibegateway.com

But a few years ago, my family and I went through some horrible times of grief and my faith was put to the test. I am a career woman with a singing ministry. I am very active in my home-church; I am a member of the choir and a worship leader. It was in July 2015 when I was in the middle of putting some finishing touches to one of my music albums that this terrible event occurred. I remember it like it was yesterday; my husband and I had just driven out to our church for my choir rehearsal with our baby girl who was 17 months old at that time. The plan was to drop me off and come back for me later that evening when the rehearsal was over.

She was the love of my life; I had so many plans for my child as she was my first, the one that opened my womb and made me a mother. I was pregnant at the time with our second child, but my connection with my daughter was beyond what I would have ever imagined. I loved her. We both did, her and I.

The affection I gave our daughter had turned her into a very social person who always loved to play with other members of our church and their kids, and on this day, she did precisely that when we arrived at the church. Before the start of our rehearsal, the kids would run around and catch some fun; they all looked forward to times like that when they could relax and play with their friends, and our daughter was no different. It was a friendly atmosphere, and we were all quite happy to meet and spend quality time together.

At some point, my husband had to leave with our daughter. I noticed she did not want to go home with him; she wanted to stay at the church with me, and I suppose she also wanted to continue playing.

It is tough for me to bring to memory the events of that evening and tell you what happened in the next hours after my husband left the church. It still feels unreal to this day, and like many people, when you revisit the events that led to the death of a loved one, you begin with hindsight to see a bigger picture and start to feel that the worst could have been avoided. I know that at this point, such feelings are completely unnecessary as we cannot turn back the hands of time, so I'll continue.

I remember vividly how much she did not want to leave and how adamant I was that she should join her father on his way home. I had another rehearsal scheduled in a different location right after the one I was in, and I knew I would not be able to handle her alone since I did not drive. As I waved them goodbye and went back into the church, I felt a heaviness in my heart that I could not explain, so I rushed out again to see if I could catch up with my husband and ask him to leave her with me since she was crying inconsolably, but they were gone.

Halfway into our choir rehearsal, I had to leave to the second rehearsal that had been scheduled. I joined another friend who was heading in the same direction. We arrived at the venue, and the rehearsal went on as planned. As we got to the end of the rehearsal, we joined our hands together to share a closing prayer. My phone rang. It was my husband calling. Once the prayer was over, I immediately called him back to know why he was calling. Apparently, he had called several times as he was trying to see if it was okay for him to come and pick me up. As I tried to reassure him that I already made arrangements with another church member to drop me at home, the unthinkable happened.

Unknown to me, on the other end and distracted by the call, my husband didn't realise that our beloved baby girl was pulling the tablecloth from the table. It was unclear if she was trying to grab something or was just holding on to the tablecloth for balance, but on that same table and on top of the tablecloth was a hot cup of tea that he had placed there to take my call.

It happened so fast. As she pulled the tablecloth, down came the mug and its content, pouring down her head, face, neck, and chest. He did not realise this had happened while he was on the call until he had ended it. I, on the other, was completely oblivious of what had happened and made my way home. As I arrived, I met a doctor friend of mine at the front door of my house. Not knowing why she was there, we both walked in together, and that was when I came face to face with the unimaginable.

We rushed her to the ER, where we were told that she had only experienced first-degree burns, even though I felt it looked worse. I was at least grateful that their report wasn't worse than what it was. She was admitted to the hospital for a total number of 6 days and Hubby, and I was there with her the entire time. Throughout those days, I kept asking the doctors why they had not administered any antibiotics, and the general answer was that it wouldn't be given unless it was vital. Little did we know that by the day we were discharged, she had developed an infection. It was lovely to be home, and I breathe a sigh of relief, not realising what was ahead of us.

Although she seemed slow from the hospital and on the way back home, she slept well that night. I just felt her slowness must be from the morphine and medicines she had been on from the hospital. Little did we know that we would be right back at that hospital a day after getting discharged. It was 9 pm. It was bad; it was terrible as I had noticed that our daughter had a hard time breathing, so we had to return to the children's hospital. When the nurses saw us, they knew it was an emergency and alerted a doctor. He checked her and tried to help her breathe, but it did not seem to work. They immediately moved us to the ICU. The doctor who took over from the previous doctor came into the room and said,
"This is going to be a very long night".

When I heard this, I immediately rejected the negative talk. The doctors came in and out, and no one was speaking to us. The entire process of attending to her was very slow, considering that it was an emergency. No one knew, not even the doctors, that she had developed Sepsis - a potentially life-threatening condition caused after developing an infection. I felt overcome by feelings of powerlessness and total disbelief. They eventually returned into the room to advise us that an x-ray was needed and there were plans being put in place to fly us to Glasgow Hospital due to the lack of ventilators in the children's hospital where we were. The doctors kept on checking her pulse and questions kept on coming:

"What happened here?"

"Has she taken antibiotics?"

What could anyone say in these circumstances?

Things went from bad to worse as the hours passed as we remained in the Intensive Care Unit of the Children's Hospital. The more we watched the doctors come and go, the more confused we were... They looked as if they did not know what to do. Overall, it did not look good for her at all.

Being a Christian and a firm believer in the power of God, when a man can do nothing more, God alone remains the most effective resort. With that in mind, I prayed. I walked and prayed in the hospital hall. Joined by another family friend who came to assist us, we walked and prayed. I was determined to let my Christian faith work. I believed God for one last miracle for my child.

She was still struggling for air, and all this time, the doctors and nurses were struggling to find any veins on her body to draw blood. It was catastrophic and confusing at the same time. At a point, the child just wanted to be carried, so her dad picked her up. While she was resting in her father's arms, she looked scared and very vulnerable. Suddenly, she started speaking with a very distinct voice, like she had seen something and was calling our attention to it, but because she was little, we could not understand what she was trying to say. She did not yet know how to talk, but we could tell she was trying to tell us something while in her father's arms. She tried to speak again and then lost consciousness. All I could hear was her father trying to revive her by screaming her name.

It was panic again in that room. The doctors rushed in and put my baby on life support, desperately trying to revive her. They tried and tried again, but she was gone. I remember the doctor coming to us and saying something like this, and I am paraphrasing:

"We cannot get a pulse. We will try just one more time, and if nothing, we would have to stop and declare her gone".

I asked them to try again. I believed God was going to bring her back. They did it one last time, and then they let go. I remember at that moment, calling out to God for her return, and the doctors all looked at me and walked out.

I think I was hoping for one last miracle because I kept on praying and singing about the goodness of God as I asked Him to intervene. I believed God could raise her, up to the day she was buried, I never let go; for God raises the dead, and I believe He still raises the dead in our days. The more I prayed, the colder she became, she was gone, but I refused to accept this. Eventually, my husband picked me up to take me home. As I left the hospital, I looked at her and called her name and told her that I would be waiting for her at home.

My beloved baby was gone, but I could not cry, I did not want to believe that this was it for her; I wanted her to breathe again; I wanted the hospital to call us back and tell us she started breathing again, that she was going to recover and that she was going to be okay.

This is just a small portion of the terrible events that have occurred in my life. Losing a child is such a terrible thing, and I wish it on nobody. As tragic as it was, I felt touched a certain way by my faith in God and the wonderful Christian community that assisted me, and still do, through those terrible days.

Therefore, I believe the right thing to do is come forward and share my story with others and perhaps use my experience to help someone else through their healing process.

In John 14:26, we are told, "The Spirit will teach you all things," and it is true. Our days of grieving might feel like the most trying times of our lives, but through my own Christian and grieving experience, I have come to realise that the Holy Spirit can work as an instructor that trains and corrects us, as long as we remain in communion with Him. We all grieve differently and that there are no right words of consolation to say to anyone who is grieving, but I believe God can show us the way if we let him in.

Chapter 2

Grief

What is Grief?

Grief is often described as deep sorrow, sometimes caused by the death of another or again, a response to the loss of someone or something that has died, to which a bond or affection was formed[1]. This definition sums up what we experience when we are grieving as we feel a deep sense of sorrow immediately after losing someone close to us. Grief is not foreign to the heart of God's children, and nothing prepares us for the rollercoaster of emotions we experience once the loss happens. Their faces will never be seen again in this life; their laughter will no longer be heard; their company will never be felt; they are gone from the land of the living. Loss is real, and so is the consequential grief associated with it.

In my case, it was a very long process. I entered a turbulent time of grieving when my daughter passed on where I lost my habits and got lost in a long and painful cycle of questioning. It was hard for me to make sense of the loss of my child, and strangely enough, I had directed all my thoughts to her, because she was the first child and the only one at the time. I dedicated all my hopes and dreams to her, and when she died, all the many plans and dreams that I had for her regarding her life and her growing up ALL CAME CRASHING DOWN.

Interestingly, it was friends and family who were most worried about my then six-months-old pregnancy, and I am so thankful that I come from a culture where people dedicate their time just to see you get better. For instance, after my daughter died, a close friend took it upon herself to come to my home and pull the curtains that I had left shut for a while. She took me to the shower, and there she consoled me. She put on replay a worship song by William McDowell - My Heart Sings. This was kept playing for hours every day.

I was broken and in such disbelief that I still could not bring myself to cry. In those times and in as much pain as I was experiencing, I still had to accommodate friends and well-wishers who came to visit and share their condolences. I also had to deal with the Police who came interrogating as part of their routine investigation, especially when the cause of death is yet to be ascertained. Many of these visits weren't the most pleasant at the time. I remember that on a particular day, as I sat on the chair, I would always sit on for hours until I had to go to bed, a couple came to visit. Usually, I sit on the chair and get left alone by anyone who would come, but this day was different. The man who had come to visit with his wife practically ordered me to go to the kitchen and find something to do as he could not understand why I was just sitting there.

As a Christian surrounded by other believers, the usual lingo would fly around from time to time, like "It is well!" or "What is done is done, it will pass!" or "You need to move on". I knew that no one could really understand what I was going through, and they only spoke based on their understanding. I was hurt

22

many of those times, and it became part of my grief. So I can attest to you that the pain that comes with grieving is very hard to bear, daily.

Looking back after all these years, I can clearly explain how it feels in the light of my own experiences. I have been able to understand grief by not only going through it but also by learning to grow despite the pain. Therefore, I can explain all these things with much clarity today.

In my attempt to explain the concept of grief with the clarity I have gained over the years, I would like us to ask ourselves with objectivity this question:

"Why is it so hard for us to let go of the people/things we love or feel attached to, once they are gone?"

I believe that the answer lies in this word: BOND.

As humans, we are created to share connections with each other and certain things around us. This bond expresses itself as an amazing feeling of affection or love that erupts once we share unforgettable moments or experiences with someone or something. No matter the person or the thing, from the moment you grow that bond, any form of separation will be very hard to handle. The case for grief becomes acceptable when we realise that it is a natural response to our experience of separation and loss.

We all live, breathe, and work hard to get those things that enrich us positively emotionally, and that is why we also work hard for these things to last. Overall, those things are conditioned by our relationships or coexistence with people or things throughout our lives. So, as soon as we lose these people or things, it feels like something has been broken or, again, something has been ripped off from us, which justifies why grieving seems to be so hard to overcome.

Another thing that we need to understand is that everyone grieves differently. Grieving is ultimately an individual process. Some people initially feel numb and disoriented, then endure pangs of yearning for the person who has died. Others feel anxious; some people have trouble sleeping. For instance, I have come across a situation where someone who was bereaved began to dwell on old arguments or words they wish they had expressed to the one who had passed. [2] Some may try to hold on to the positive memories for a while to celebrate the Person they just lost, while others would want to spend some time alone to cry and try to make some sense out of the sad event that just occurred. Sudden outbursts of tears are common in grief, triggered by memories of the loved one. Even those who are confident, that their loved one is with the Lord, still struggle with sadness over their loss.

Not all people grieve the same way or for the same amount of time. Some people grieve for a short period of time, while others grieve for years. I could see this difference in grieving, even with my husband. Although I cannot deny that we have both suffered during this horrible experience, he *seemed* to cope much better than I did. For instance, he could get back to work shortly after losing our child, which I could not understand, even though I could not bring myself to believe that he did not care or that he had put it all behind him. She died in his arms, and it was his scream that alerted the doctors who came rushing in the room to save her. She was his child as much as she was mine, but our different methods of grieving were evident and his strength and ability to recover played a huge role in helping me survive, as it also played a great role in saving our marriage.

In times of loss, our dealing with our grief is essential in order for us to come to terms with our loss and move forward with our lives. To do this, we must be honest in your grieving and ask God the tough questions that we would normally be too scared to ask.

The Grieving Process and How to Understand It

An English hymn writer known as William Cowper said, "Grief is itself a medicine." People may say, "Don't cry; your loved one is in heaven." [3] That may be true, but it is also imperative to deal with the actual pain of loss. We should never feel guilty for grieving because it is a required part of God's pathway to healing.

Grieving is like sailing across a stormy sea. When we first experience a significant loss, it launches us into a cyclone of emotions. We feel surrounded by darkness and heavy waves of anguish. It drowns comforting words by hurricane-force winds of sorrow. We feel lonely and out of control as it sweeps us toward uncharted paths.

Stages of Grieving

Looking back with more clarity, one of the things that I have learned through my ordeal is that grieving is also a process. What this means is that there are several stages to go through, what I choose to call the stages of grieving, that will finally take you to the final point of recovery. This starts from the *acknowledgement* of an unexpected loss - where someone you love suddenly dies; or an unacceptable loss - where there is a knowledge of impending death with the hope of it not happening, to an *acceptance* of the loss - where one accepts the implications associated with the loss, and then to a point where they *accommodate* the loss – a phase of letting go or moving forward with life in spite of the loss.

Several people do find it hard to get to the place of acknowledgement, where the journey to recovery begins. They remain in a position of shock and sorrow and mostly denial. When this is not handled properly, they can start to regress and fall into depression and have series of emotional outbursts. Their anger may be directed towards family, friends, doctors, the one who died or even at God. Other typical feelings include lethargy, apathy, and guilt over perceived failures or unresolved personal issues. This is why it is so important to understand the process of grieving for ourselves, and as we assist those who find themselves in the place of loss.

Within all the stages of grieving, people go through a number of phases, and in no particular order, I'll explain these phases as I experienced them:

The Phase of Shock

The phase of shock usually occurs when one first receives bad news. Here you are in a state of disbelief and may start having some physical responses like increased heart rate, uncontrollable shaking, loss of speech, fainting, uncontrollable crying and screaming etc. In the days and weeks following a devastating loss, common feelings include numbness and looking lost, like one is trapped in a bad dream. These manifestations are not necessarily common to all of us, and while crying is the most common manifestation of mourning, people may react differently when they have just heard the news of the passing of a loved one. For me, this stage was strange because my state of shock did not find its expression in tears. For a long time, I could not bring myself to shed a tear. I would describe myself at this point as someone who was in complete denial of what had just happened.

The Phase of Inconsolable Sorrow

As the reality of the loss begins to set in, we are overcome by a deep sense of sorrow; this is usually accompanied by Weeping and other forms of emotional trauma. The feeling of loneliness and depression may also occur. The stage of uncontrollable sorrow comes after one realises that the Person with which a tight bond has been shared will never return. Here, your body feels like it is shutting down, and you have a hard time sleeping or eating. If it is the loss of a parent, lover or carer, you might begin to feel quite insecure, exposed, lost and afraid. As you bring to memory the beautiful times shared with the one you have lost, the pain increases, and you might feel even more shattered. When I reached this phase in my moments of grief, I did not want to do anything; the pain immobilised me as I sat on the same chair every day, lost in my thoughts. The idea that the child I had given birth to, nurtured and cared for all those months would never be seen again, or carried, or loved and cared for by me shattered me to my core. I never thought I could be consoled, no matter who tried to.

The Questioning Phase

Another phase comes with a lot of questioning. This time, you are trying to make sense of everything happening around you. Your mind is trying to put all the pieces together by retracing the last moments you spent with the one you lost, the last words you exchanged to see if there could have been a sign or some kind of clue that might have signalled you to expect the end. Perhaps at this stage, you may try to rationalise your loss by attaching it to something else that you can reconcile. This is a very normal thing to do for most of us, as we live in a rational world where most concepts need to be palpable or verifiable. We want everything to make sense to us one way or the other. In my case, I remained in this phase for a very long time. I questioned everything the happened around me, from the inception of my grieving to the moment I gave birth to my second child three months later and afterwards. I questioned everything. I couldn't understand how a child as little as mine could go through that much suffering to the point of death and nothing could be done to save her. My questioning was directed at every party involved, including myself, and I didn't know where to stop.

The Phase of Depression

One of the most delicate phases one might expression is the phase of depression. Many people would keep themselves at this stage because they are having a hard time overcoming the pain. This is a very dangerous phase for mental health and can be a life-changing one, as people who linger into depression seem to have given up on hope, happiness, their daily routines, and everything that would normally give them a reason to be themselves and live a purposeful life. I talk about this now with much clarity, but it was not always this way. The depression that emerged from grieving my child had some very disastrous effects on me, my marriage, and to some extent, the baby I gave birth to 3 months after losing my daughter. Losing a child while expecting another one is really messed up, and in my case, I had often felt bad for the other child because I did not have the capacity to give her the attention she deserved when she was in my womb. I was broken, angry, and depressed and had no strength nor will to do what I would have usually done while pregnant. Without the right kind of help, a lot of people remain in this phase for such a long time with adverse effects. It is imperative that everyone going through this phase are exposed to the right kind of help that will get them out.

The Phase of Realisation

This phase often precedes overcoming the phase of depression. This doesn't just happen, and as already mentioned above, the right kind of help is very necessary for anyone to get to this phase. At this point, you begin to accept your loss, and you finally realise that there is life ahead of you. You acknowledge that the love and bond you shared with the one you have lost cannot be taken away even though they are gone, and you begin to cherish the good memories and the impact made by the one you had lost when they were alive. From my experience, I can tell you that my stage of realisation was a very gradual one considering the circumstances of my loss. As the years passed, other wonderful things began to happen to my husband and me. It was hard at first. Once my second child was born, I became more paranoid because I was scared to lose her too. I did not want random people around her, and everything little things that happened to her freaked me out that I was always on calls to health services and other professionals like my sister who is a paediatrician in the USA. Ten months after my baby was born, I got pregnant again, and I looked forward to having that child. But unfortunately, three months into the pregnancy, I suffered a miscarriage. I became angrier and felt I was being attacked. All this anger, as you can imagine, led to quarrels between my husband and me and my family at large. I place all these events in the realisation phase for me because it was within these events that, with the help of my family and friends and also with more children on the way, I slowly began to realise that there was a life ahead for me and

I could not stay stuck in what had now become my past. Even though I felt broken, my children still needed my love and attention, and so did my husband. Despite our loss, we never gave up on having more kids as we desired to have three children. We picked it up and kept going with the hope that one day at a time, things would get better.

The Recovery Phase

This is the most promising phase in the stages of grief as there is finally a gradual and almost noticeable return to normalcy. This is a time of adjustment, as you begin to accommodate the new normal of the absence of the Person, you have lost. Here, you begin to realise that they would never have wanted you to be sad for such a long time and would want you to move forward with your life and succeed. Many people begin to respond with gratitude for the times they were opportune to spend with their loved one. In this phase, your positive attitude is probably the key to why you begin to feel stronger and more confident about what is to come than in any other phase you might have experienced. I can tell you that it took a long time for me to get to this phase, but with friends and family around and with the Holy Spirit staying close to me, and my husband and I resolving to work hand in hand through our pain, soon enough the wound in my heart began to heal. At this stage, you end up reconnecting with reasons to enjoy life and feel more grateful for what you still have in your life.

It is important to note that these phases do not happen consecutively. An individual may go through all or may experience only a few. These phases will also vary in duration for each Person, so we must try not to impose a timetable on anyone. Healing does take time. Healing a broken heart is like healing a broken leg. Removing a cast before the bone is strong enough to bear weight will hinder long-term recovery. So, it is with the healing of our hearts. Unresolved grief may trigger depression, alcoholism, drug abuse, or other serious problems. Over time, the strength of your grief will diminish, but it is important not to rush the grieving process.

Non-Progressive Phase

If you are attending to someone who is overtaken by grief and who does not seem to heal from that pain, it is important to know the symptoms that show that they have remained in a non-progressive phase. In my case, I was predominantly overtaken by anger. I was just always angry, replaying the scenes, questioning the doctors' decisions on that day, and blaming myself for not deciding to keep her with me during rehearsal. I remained in this state for a very long while, and I felt like no one could get me out or offer the help that I needed. I felt stuck. When we come in contact with situations like these, knowing the symptoms will help us know what sort of assistance is required, especially when their health is on the line.

For those who are grieving, it is also important to know when you have gotten to a point where you are not making any progress. Identifying these symptoms would allow you the opportunity to know when to ask for help. The people around you can offer more guidance on how to face the tough times you are going through. Now, I was not great at opening up to my family, and most of it had to do with the fact that I felt they just did not understand what I was going through. But some saw the signs and began to reach out in a way that helped me open. Therefore, it is important to understand the symptoms.

Emotional/ Physical and Cognitive Symptoms of Non-Progressive Phase

Below are some of the symptoms that may manifest in someone who has not made much progress in their grieving phases:

Constant Sad Demeanor

A person grieving may have a very sad face, with circles around his/her eyes because of lack of sleep, or even puffy eyes because they constantly cry, which is normal. If you notice that this is more regular, it is probably a symptom that they are stuck in a phase.

Dark Thoughts and Words

Being traumatised by a person's death can make you feel lost, which may lead you to see the world with a lot of negativity. In my case, it was mostly anger and withdrawal that I would then transfer to my family.

Excessive Lamentation

Here, the Person grieving may complain too much about the world, their fate and the unfairness of life in general. They may present their tragedy as the most horrible thing the world has ever seen, which, to be fair is the case when you lose a loved one. Yet the excessive act of lamenting can make them seem like they are seeking attention or desperately wanting to be seen as a victim.

Constantly Lost in Thought

A person who is possibly stuck in a phase might most times look 'absent', and you can tell that this person is not who they used to be. For me, I sat in the same spot in our living room for a while. Every time we would get visitors, they would just find me at the same spot, totally absent in thought, drowned in my sorrow.

Constantly Unhappy and Unmotivated

When someone is non-progressive, they plunge easily into a phase of deep depression, where being active and showing signs of happiness is almost impossible because they do not have the mental strength to do and enjoy certain things anymore. I am sure at some point that people thought I was weak and refusing to move on as I let my child's death affect my work, my faith, and my family life.

Increased Desire to Remain Secluded

People who grieve spend most of their time secluded in their room. They prefer to be alone. This was mostly true, especially since I was trying to avoid exposing myself to the things that hurt me.

Slow or Fast Degradation in Health

For people who already have health problems, going through periods of grief can worsen things because the emotion of sadness might be too much for them to handle. As I previously mentioned, I gave birth a few months after losing my first child. I was still in shock and refusing to let go, and I believe this increased the difficulty I faced in my pregnancy and caused a very difficult recovery afterwards.

Fear and Loneliness While Grieving

I realise how much of a mystery it might be to those who witness the degradation of the mental state of a person who is grieving, as they seem lost, lonely and scared in a new world of sadness. In this world, a lot of negative things thrive, like insomnia, hallucination, the refusal to eat, which leads to malnutrition which can spiral down to an uncontrollable mess.

One of the other reasons for fear and loneliness while grieving is closely linked to the Christian context to which I found myself. The notion that a Christian isn't supposed to mourn for long and should move on quickly has caused a lot of pain to those who have had cause for grieving.

There are many other reasons why people feel fearful and lonely in their grief. The feeling that people sometimes do not understand their pain, especially when they are told to move on while the pain is still palpable in their hearts drives them to a place of isolation.

The feeling that everyone else is moving on with their lives, laughing, smiling, and spending time with their loved ones while they feel stuck in their pain is also a cause for loneliness and fear. For someone who is grieving, it may feel like mental torture to see everyone else happy while they are sad.

Perhaps the feeling of suddenly being vulnerable, especially if this Person gave you strength, motivated you, and was always by your side, can cause a profound sense of fear once they are gone.

Also, one may now have a fear of dying too, because losing someone very close to you and seeing this Person lie in a casket and put underground makes you realise that one day this might be you. For me, the feeling of seeing death everywhere was palpable, especially when my second child was born. I was so paranoid and scared that the same thing might happen to her that I made sure that I was extra careful with who came around her. Overnight I changed from a smiling and bubbly gospel artist to an unhappy, withdrawn, and angry Person.

There are many ways to handle grief with more bravery and face it with more character, and there is no doubt that observing and understanding God's way of doing things through the Holy Spirit could be the way. But let us not suffocate our pain as Christians, we must give ourselves time to heal. I do not believe people should hide and ignore their pain, because in my case, the pain helped me grow and even reinforced my faith in God. I would say that embracing your pain and taking every opportunity to open about how you feel in that very instant can help you deal with the different stages and phases of grieving. Also, surrounding yourself with support networks or people who have been where you find yourself at the moment also helps.

Overall, grief is something that we all go through in our lives, and we will have our ways to cope with it, but it is an overly complicated thing to go through. Understanding the stages, phases and symptoms that show when someone is stuck will go a long way to help the healing process.

Chapter 3

God and Grieving

For a lot of people, religion can be an incredible source of comfort in times of loss. It is said that religion is a source to help provide meaning and answers to the problems of uncertainty, powerlessness, and scarcity that death creates.[2] While many earthly religions attempt to answer the questions that arise in the face death, only the Christian faith provides the absolute truth that brings the greatest source of hope in times of loss.

The Bible in Ecclesiastes 3:4 (NRSV) says, "There is a time to weep, and a time to laugh; a time to mourn, and a time to dance". God's word in the Holy Bible and the Christian faith gives us great hope in the face of loss, It does not rescue us from the pain of loss, nevertheless, deep faith in Christ infuses our grief with hope.

As believers, loss can cause us to question our faith in God as we struggle to make sense of death. Grief can blur our feelings about our faith, and our faith can confuse our feelings about

---

[2] Ekore RI, Lanre-Abass B. African cultural concept of death and the idea of advance care directives. Indian J Palliat Care 2016;22:369-72

our grief, but the depth of your grief does not imply a loss of faith.

Grief is not foreign to the heart of God's children. Grief is a suitable response to death, even for a believer. As William Miller attests, "Crying does not brand a griever as being weak and without faith"[3]. It is ok for you to cry. It is ok to experience and express feelings of anger in grief. These feelings are come natural to humans and don't make you a bad person.

I entered a turbulent time of grieving when my daughter died. Nothing prepares us for the rollercoaster of emotions we will experience once the loss happens. Just like to everyone else, to a believer grief is real. In the scriptures, many people grieved the death of their loved ones. In fact, it was part of the custom of the children of Israel to allocate a specific number of days for a period of grieving. Traditional Jewish customs included a special meal, grieving with family and friends, prayers, and Torah readings. Normal life stopped until the period of mourning was over.

1 Thessalonian 4:13-14 says, "And regarding the question, friends, that has come up about what happens to those already dead and buried, we don't want you in the dark any longer. First off, you must not carry on over them like people who have nothing to look forward to, as if the grave were the last word. Since Jesus died and broke loose from the grave, God

---

[3] Miller, William A. *When going to Pieces Holds You Together*. Minneapolis: Augsburg, 1976.

will bring back to life those who died in Jesus," (TPT Translation)

From the Bible, God does not say we should not grieve, He only reminds us not to grieve like the world does. How does the world grieve? Like people without hope of eternal life. For those who do not believe in life after death, they think death is the end of everything. But for Christians, death is only a transition from one life to the other. The promise of eternal life in Jesus is the hope every believer holds to even in the face of death.

Also, amidst our grief, Psalm 34:18 reminds us that the Lord is near to the heartbroken and he saves the crushed in spirit. During the pain, the ache and the tears, God is near. When my daughter passed on and when I had a miscarriage, I felt God's presence close; I cannot explain it, but it was real. The only reason it felt ineffective in the sense is my refusal to accept it as the solution; I just wanted my baby back. I wanted someone to tell me it was all a dream. I can vividly remember when we went to bury her. I felt such an unexplainable peace and a nudge she was fine. I knew God was near even though I didn't suppress my sense of loss. But whether I chose to accept it or not, God's peace was all over me, and I know that I survived the entire ordeal because of His peace.

Therefore, we must realise that we are never left to grieve alone. God promised in his word that He is always with us and that promise is right at the core of the Christian faith. He is familiar with suffering" and "acquainted with grief" as Isaiah described him as the "man of sorrows" in Isaiah 53:3. In John

11:35, we see that Jesus wept because of the death of his friend, Lazarus. In the garden of Gethsemane, Jesus grieved as he looked ahead to the suffering that would befall him. In the face of death, he was consumed with deep sorrow. On the cross, Jesus experienced the height of grief as he cried out to the Father asking why he was forsaken? Jesus surely is acquainted with our grief and he understands.

When our grief is incapacitating and it feels impossible to function, God does not sit aloof in heaven. He does not leave us to figure out how to handle grief on our own or to wander about in search of resources to get through it. He walks with us every step of the way. He is not insusceptible or indifferent to grief and even though He does not always tell us why we are suffering, He offers himself to us as a remedy to our malady: "The Father of all compassion and the God of all comfort, who comforts us in all our troubles" 2 Corinthians 1:3–4 (NKJV). God also offers comfort in times of bereavement. Jesus said, "I will not leave you comfortless: I will come to you" John 14:18 (NKJV)

Grieving is a process that teaches us how to surrender our painfully to God so He can heal our hearts. In my grief, one thing that became real to me as time went by was the fact that no one who dies in Him really dies. One day, we will all be together with the Lord for eternity, and this is where we should find hope.

Faith Communities and Grieving

I believe faith communities should be a place of comfort and support in times of loss, and many are. In my case, I experienced great support from my faith community, and I consider myself blessed. Unfortunately, there are some that do not provide the necessary support. Consumed by the idea that faith and grief cannot co-exist, they approach those who grieve with judgment and criticism. This leaves those who grieve feeling unloved and misunderstood as they are not allowed to freely express their emotions.

I also believe that it might be unreasonable to expect everyone in an entire congregation to give you the necessary support that you need or respond to you in the way that would generally uplift you or make you feel safe to freely express yourself. Not everyone will have an ample understanding to deal with those who are grieving, and that is okay. I would suggest that you find within your community a few people who can support you. If that also proves unsuccessful, it may be worth reaching out to others with a similar faith background who have also experienced losses. It is very important to find the people and places that allow you to do that.

The truest friends and "helpers" are those who wait for the griever to emerge from the darkness that swallowed them alive without growing anxious or impatient. They do not pressure their friend to be the old familiar person they are used to; they will accept that things are different, embrace the now-scarred one they love and are confident that their compassionate, non-

demanding presence is the surest expression of God's mercy to their suffering friend. They're ok with messy and slow and few answers.... and they never say, "Move on." - Kay and Rick Warren[4]

Culture and Grieving

Born and raised in a Christian community that share a similar cultural background, I realise there is a silent community voice that suggests to the bereaved person that they to contain their sorrow. I have seen this play out many times while growing up, and because of this voice, a lot of people form a habit of suppressing their emotions as a coping mechanism. This façade is often mistaken for deep faith. A lot of people who do this are commended for being strong or tough, but I think that this flattery only helps to strengthen an unpleasant habit rather than inspire faith.

While grieving my child, I, at a point, felt alienated by my community. This was not because they did not want me around. Not at all. They had good intentions. The only reason I felt this way was because a number of the people I encountered seemed by their responses to expect me to get over my pain and just miraculously recover.

The culture in which we live or the one we were born into exerts a profound influence on our approach to grieving. A

---

[4]Grief and Faith: the relationship between belief and grief and March 12, 2014, Don't tell me to Move on- Kays Blog

culture will view death and grieving from any of these 3 perspectives:

1. Accept
2. Defy
3. Deny

From the experiences I've had with the culture, I was raised in, grieving the loss of a child is frowned at. You are to portray strength to everyone around you and show no form of weakness. I got married into a different culture than the one I was born into and found out that within this parents are not expected to outlive their children. It is also considered an abomination for parents to attend the burial of their child, and this was what was expected of me. I find that this has worked for some people but made matters worse for most. I have seen situations where some folks I know denied and ignored expressing their pain only to be affected adversely much later. Some became paranoid about everything, and some did not heal.

For my sanity, I needed to attend my daughter's funeral at the cemetery irrespective of the silent nudge not to go. I am confident to say that this helped me a lot in my process of healing. It was difficult, but I felt peace as I watched her body and the coffin lowered into the ground. I had no words to say but in my heart, the words of a song by Matt Redman kept on playing . . .

"You give and take away, You give and take away, my heart will choose to say Lord blessed be your name" [5]

I cannot predict the future, but from every indication, I presume that I might have struggled greatly with the acceptance of my child's death if I never got to see her buried: it was my moment of closure.

This was my experience, and I acknowledge that it might be totally different for others who have gone through the same. It is good for everyone to understand how they can best handle their grieving process irrespective of the cultural limitations that might exist around you. Healing is a process and we must take it one step at a time.

---

[5] Blessed Be the name of the Lord: Matt Redman

Chapter 4

Living Through Grief

When a loved one dies, a vacuum is left behind, which creates an entirely new environment around the one who is grieving. One of the most challenging tasks for a bereaved person is adjusting to that new environment. In making this adjustment, there is no rule book. Who is to say when it is okay to put away the personal effects of a loved one? Who is to say when it is appropriate to make lifestyle changes and form new relationships? Who decides when it's okay for you to put away photos and memorabilia's, or if you should at all?

When there are many people involved in the grieving process, it becomes even more complicated. One Person might be okay with a decision while the other person might not have reached that stage. When our baby girl died, her photograph was immediately taken down from our living room. This was one of those decisions that were torn between two parties. One party felt that taking the photos down was best for them and the other party didn't feel it was time to do that. Finding a middle ground will help all parties in their grieving process. The temptation to be selfish in these times will arise, but we must realise that because we are not alone, we must put others into consideration.

When I realised that the photographs were going to be taken down, I saved her photos on my phone and left it on my profile.

This remained for a very long time until I felt I was ready to take it down – for me, this was the middle ground.

When it came to other personal effects like her clothes and the things in her room, I touched nothing. I couldn't step into her room until three months after when I knew my baby was due. I remember like it was yesterday when friends came to help me out as I moved and re-arranged the room to get it ready for the new baby. But a few years later, I realised that I was always very sad and the house we lived in held too many bad memories and I needed a new start, so we moved to a new home.

None of all of these happened at the same time. We dealt with each feeling and decision as they presented themselves. There is no need to rush the process using the rule book of other people's expectations. As we trust God through your grieving process, He will reveal the timing and the direction we must take.

Managing Grief – Lessons Learned

One of the reasons I decided to write this book is to share the lessons I learned through my time of grieving. I believe our pain and scars are not meant to be hidden, but we can teach good lessons to others from what we have been through. These are some of the lessons I learned to help you as you try to manage grief.

Things May Get Worse But it Will Get Better: Do Not Lose Hope.

When my daughter Aanu died, I thought that the first few weeks would be the worst and that the struggle would wane as the weeks progressed. I was wrong. I came to realise I was in shock for the first few months. With each passing day, I gained an increasing awareness of the immense magnitude of pain that came with her death. I was even more miserable from the third through the seventh month than I was in the first month.

It is not abnormal if you feel that as time progresses, you still feel very sad. There is no shame in the grieving process. Your acknowledgement, acceptance and accommodation of your loss are most paramount. Acceptance involves overcoming the natural denial response. This happened to me during the funeral when I witnessed the casket being laid into the ground. For someone else, this can be facilitated by viewing the body after death, attending funeral and burial services, and visiting the place where the body is laid to rest. In addition, talking about the deceased person or the circumstances of the death can be very helpful.

It is essential to grieve the physical implications of losing a loved one, and it is important to come to grips with the fact that you will not see that person again in this life. But if your loved one died in Christ, you can be certain that you will see them again in heaven, and this is our hope.

There Is No Shortcut: Recovery Goes Through The Pain

The first few years after my daughter died, I allowed myself to grieve. I made space for it and accepted reality. It was a difficult thing to do, but going through the pain was the only way I could start taking the small strides to move forward.

Let's look at this analogy for a moment; if your knee is going to heal after a sports injury, you're going to have to do the painful work that comes with rehabilitation. If you're going to get stronger, you're going to have to experience the soreness that comes from workouts. If a broken bone is going to heal, you're going to have to endure the pain of setting the bone.[9]

So, is it with grief? The way to restoration is through the pain. Allow yourself to feel the sadness, and with each tear, you cry; you are moving closer to healing. God provides the grace we need to weather the storms of our grief, and His presence will never leave us, no matter what.

When You Can't, God Can, Just Cry Out!

Going to a counsellor, journaling your thoughts and talking about the loss, are all good in the process, but I learned that the most helpful place I could ever go-to for my healing was to Jesus. We don't have the capacity to mend our hearts, but God can. God is a Healer and Redeemer. In all the sorrow and confusion, our hope in grief lies in the reality that God can restore anything. Do not hide your emotions; when you are struggling, run to the one who knows you completely. It is never hopeless to cry out to Him. He has the power to bring hope and rest to your soul in ways you could never conceive. God, in His grace, has assigned this job to Himself.

Reinvest in Relationships

I advise that if you can, take the emotional energy you would have spent on the one who died and reinvest it in another relationship or relationships. This may be difficult for some because they might feel a sense of disloyalty or unfaithfulness for withdrawing emotionally from the one they lost. The aim is not to forget your loved one, but to finally reach a point where you can remember them without experiencing disabling grief.

There are many reasons why reinvesting time in friendships is essential. For instance, friends can give you the encouragement you need and the support needed to rebuild your life. Some people find that getting involved in a volunteering system provides structure, a sense of purpose, and built-in companionship. Others swap phone numbers with new friends from grief-recovery groups. I also realise that many surviving spouses enjoy focusing more time and energy on children, grandchildren, and great-grandchildren. For me, I connected with a few friends that I knew I could have a conversation with. While I refrained from attending parties and the likes, I could go out for a cup of coffee and have a conversation with these friends. This was my way of making use of the support network I had, and I found it quite refreshing.

Find an Outlet

Some people find they can connect with books and this can be very helpful. I could not read any book in the initial stages. All I could do was listen to music, which is another way some people find relief. As time went on, I sat and watched mind engaging movies or series. Before long, I started seeking people who had gone through similar experiences just to see how they survived. Eventually, I started searching the bible for references to words like comfort or hope. As I looked up the verses, I meditated on each one and record them in a prayer journal. Soon enough, God's healing words began to sink in. Psalm 94:19 says, "In the multitude of my anxieties within me, Your comforts delight my soul" (NKJV).

The pain of grief can be very intense, and there arises a tendency to run away from it. Many people drown themselves in drugs, alcohol, and many forms of addiction to numb the pain, but running from it is not the solution. Our outlets must be a channel to embrace our pain, not run from it. This is the road to survival.

Offer Support in Spite of Your Differences

Loss shapes the future of families and individuals. Its impact depends on actions or inactions.

I realise that everyone grieves differently. It is a very individual process and can be an incredibly lonely journey. I also realise that men and women also deal with loss differently. I discovered this with my husband and me and from research. Men want to move on, to make plans, to focus on new horizons. Women want to spend more time remembering the person who has died; they want to immerse themselves in pain. It is important to say here that we can learn from each other. You should have the time when you grieve and the time when you take a break from the grief. Finding a healthy balance between the two is very necessary.

I believe that men and women can help one another. This is even more crucial with a man and his wife or partner when dealing with the loss of a child. The man can help the woman in the times when she needs to take a break from drowning in the pain, by taking her for a walk in the park or going on a road trip or other forms of excursions. The woman can help the man in encouraging him to express how he feels and let out the pain he might be bottling up.

It is a very difficult time when multiple people have to go through grief triggered by the same event and have to grieve differently. It took me a while to understand this, and this led to a turbulent time in my home. The most efficient way to deal with this is by being open in communicating how you are feeling to others in your family. "The families that cope well are those who can share their feelings openly. Death disrupts the complex and finely tuned balance in a family, so everything has to be reorganised – and being open helps with that process." [10]

Seek Help or Support

God made you exceptional, and your grieving process will be an individual journey. But keep in mind that the weight of grief is lighter when shared. Support from others can help you handle the aftermath of your loss. When your heart is breaking, and your eyes are blinded by grief, you need the help of others more than ever.[11]

During my time of grieving, I was referred to a counsellor because I was pregnant with our second child and also showed signs of depression, which was not good for the unborn child and me. Therapy was helpful. When I was home, I stayed mute most of the time, but at my sessions, I could freely express myself to someone who was disposed to listening to me.

But counselling was not the only thing that helped me open up. I began to draw closer to another Christian mother who like myself had lost a child. Spending time with her helped because I felt we shared common feelings and could exchange them without being judgmental. I am forever grateful for having met her because I found a lot of healing flow from our discussions, prayers, and relationship over the years.

As I look back, I feel so blessed to have had all these options at hand: friends, family, and even people at my job who cared enough to assist me and recommend solutions along the way.

So, I would recommend to anyone going through grief to consider reaching out for help from the following:

Friends:

Friends are ideal under these circumstances, and real friends will always show up with help. They can help in so many ways, like assisting with shopping for groceries, or cooking when you've run out of food, or just to make you smile when you need cheering up.

Pastoral support:

I am blessed to be serving under a pastor who is a true father to me. At various times, he would check upon us, and all he did was listen to me pour out my heart, and then he will pray with us. I regained a lot of my strength from times like those. If you can, I would advise that you seek godly pastoral/spiritual support.

Family:

Family members bring us unconditional love and maybe the first ones at the scene in times of pain. When you feel depressed, you sometimes lose touch with that unconditional connection, and through prayer, you can finally reopen your heart to the most important members of your family.

Support Group:

Support groups are where people with similar issues meet and share their stories. These Meetings help to deal with feelings of fear and isolation. The knowledge that other people are going through the same symptoms, phases and stages will remind you that you are not alone and that what you are going through is normal. In these meeting, attendees rally around each other to provide the much need support to get through it.

Individual Therapy:

If and where possible, it is very important to seek therapy with a godly counsellor.

Supporting Someone Grieving

It is a very complicated maze to navigate through while trying to support someone who is grieving. It is so easy to say and do the wrong things, and because a lot of people are not informed about how to handle such a delicate situation like grieving, they find themselves on the wrong side of those they are trying to offer support to.

Unfortunately, I sadly had to make a difficult decision to withdraw from several people who I felt at the time surrounded me with much negativity. Instances like I mentioned earlier about the man who asked that I occupy myself in the kitchen, and times when people compared my loss of a child to the loss of a job, terminal illness and fertility issues in their bid to get me to see the reason why I shouldn't feel bad, all left a sour taste in my mouth. I broke down in tears a number of times in response to words that lacked comfort, and my natural response was then to withdraw.

This is why I say that offering support to someone who is grieving is a very tricky maze to navigate through. Hence, there are a few things that I can share from my experience that will guide anyone who is looking to be a source of support and comfort to those who is grieving.

- Ask God for guidance about what to say and when to say it. God is a God of comfort, and His words are gentle and healing. If we choose to speak as we are led by Him, our words will bring the necessary healing that we seek. The bible admonishes us to not lean on our own understanding but to trust the Lord to direct our path. I believe that that admonition applies in offering comfort to others.

-Be a friend that is observant and one that listens. Be prepared to recognise the extent of your friend's loss by sitting in silence with them. This will give them the opportunity to express themselves or not, whatever their choice is. Allowing the griever to be upset, confused, contradictory or silent will help you know where you need to step in.

- There is a subtle tendency to preach at people who are grieving. From my experience, it can be quite distasteful as much as the intentions might be good. When people are in their initial stages of grief, it is best to stay clear of telling them what you think they should do to feel better as you might not understand exactly how they feel.

- It is best to avoid clichés and Christianise. It is very important to allow the griever come to terms with their grief without making them question their own spirituality by using phrases like "Cheer up", "Be joyful in the Lord" or "It is well".

- Prayer is such an important tool for bringing comfort. Unfortunately, it can also be amiss. As we pray for those who grieve, we must remember that aim of our prayers is for the Lord to bring comfort through the pain and not magically take the pain away by some means of substitution.

- It is okay to cry around those who are grieving, especially if you genuinely feel the pain that they feel and if they are crying too. Jesus wept with Mary and Martha at the death of Lazarus.

- **Be there for the long haul.** Remember to make contact and be supportive after everyone else has gone. Usually, a few months after the tragedy, people go back to their normal lives as they should. But for the one who is grieving, it is far from over. Sending a text or paying a visit can go a long way in offering comfort.

-Sending letters, cards, texts, or emails are extremely helpful.

- **Practical help can never be overstated.** Do simple things without being asked, such as bringing a meal or mowing the lawn. Doing practical things are often what makes a difference. Do something helpful for those who cannot attend to those things at the time will leave a lasting effect in their hearts.

Helpful Things To Say [12]

- I cannot imagine how you feel

- I cannot imagine how painful/devastating/heart-breaking this has been for you

- There are no words; I don't know what to say.

- Ask "what happened?" in order to give them the chance to talk. Do not be tempted to fix them the problem; offer only a listening ear.

- Stay in the moment as they speak. If your mind wanders, they will know, and you will become an unsafe space. Be empathetic. This means that you are allowed to tear up during their story.

Though these points are not all-encompassing, I believe that careful consideration of these will go a long way as we try to offer comfort to each other in our communities.

Forgiveness

For those who are bereaved, the tendency to be offended when someone steps on a raw nerve by saying or doing something inappropriate is very common. Many who come to offer comfort do it because they care, and though they might not have the right words or the right attitude, we must not allow their imperfections cause us more grief as we give room for error and forgive every display of ignorance.

Forgiveness is very important as holding a grudge can hinder your recovery process. It is scientifically proven that those who let go easily recover much quicker than those who harbour anger within them. So, for the sake of yourself, it is always best to be quick to forgive those who hurt you while you are grieving.

Grief Recovery

What does recovery mean? Recovery from loss is achieved by a series of small and correct choices made by the griever. Sadly, most of us have not been given the information with which to make correct choices in response to a loss. Recovery means feeling better. Recovery is you discovering new meaning for living without the fear of being hurt again.[13] Recovery is being able to enjoy fond memories without reliving the painful past. Recovery is acknowledging that it is perfectly alright to feel sad from time to time and to talk about those feelings, no matter how those around you react. Recovering from significant emotional loss is not a straightforward task, and it is not true that time heals all wounds as time does not possess such powers. Taking the actions that lead to recovery will require the open-mindedness, willingness, and courage of the Person grieving, and I believe that as we consider the points that have been raised with respect to my experience, it'll be easier to move forward on the journey of recovery.

Chapter 5

The Healing Power of God's Word

In the initial months of my daughter passing away, I lost the strength and the will to do anything. Everything in my life seemed to lie dormant; cooking, cleaning, praying and even reading my bible. Fortunately, my love for music was the window that allowed a ray of hope through my shattered heart. Every day, worship songs would play in my room non-stop, and the words of the songs that played encouraged me as much as they could.

After a while, I began to listen to sermons on the internet, and I prayed a lot in the spirit. I also began to hear verses of scripture drop in my heart, and right then I knew that I had received some strength to pick up my bible again, and as I responded to that strength welling up inside of me, my spirit came alive again.

God's word is a compass that helps us navigate through the dark tunnel of life's troubles.

The entrance of Your words gives light; It gives understanding to the simple. Psalm 119:130 NKJV

From my experience, I can say that God's word-finding a place in my heart gave me the strength I needed to begin picking up the pieces of my life. God used this word to encourage me that He has got my back, and this gave me some comfort.

Life may be unpredictable; God's Word is an anchor for our souls. It is His words that make us steadfast and enables us to withstand the weight of anything that tries to crush our faith. The bible is God's word to you, no matter what you face along the way. Always remember there is a specific word for every situation you pass through. There is something very significant about God's word. It heals wounds. His word is alive and carries life.

I remember taking one of my children to the hospital for a scheduled surgery. Once he was put to sleep, I was asked to return to the ward to wait. This is because surgeries are done in the confines of the theatre where everything is prepared for such a delicate operation. Only a select few are allowed when a surgery is being performed. I use this analogy to explain that there are seasons in our lives when God will require us to be alone with Him as He does delicate work in our hearts. In seasons like these, His word builds us up and heals us to the utmost.

I remember that season God brought me into this lonely place of encounter. My anger was redirected, and I rose to resist the devil. I couldn't sit down and watch my life fall apart. With the strength I received, I started praying and digging into the word. It was in this season that God showed to me the state of my heart and the things that need to be healed and the things I needed to let go.

In our place of grief, we must run to the word of God; it is the anchor for our souls. When we dwell on the word of God, a number of things happen as a result:

1. The word of God reveals to us who God is.

In His Word, we find the truth that will set us free from every bondage that will try to hold us down. As God reveals Himself to us through His Word, we are confident to trust in His power to heal and restore us.

"I am the LORD, the God of all the peoples of the world. Is anything too hard for me? Jeremiah 32:27 (NLT)

2. The word of God reveals the plans of God to us.

God exposes His plans for our lives in His word. When we dig deep into the bible, we find all His promises concerning us, and as we trust and believe them, we are strengthened.

"Remember the former things of old, For I am *God, and* there is *no other;* **I am** *God, and* **there is** *none like Me, declaring the end from the beginning, And from ancient times* **things** *that are not* **yet** *done, saying, 'My counsel shall stand, And I will do all My pleasure,' calling a bird of prey from the east, the man who executes My counsel, from a far country. I have spoken* **it;** *I will also bring it to pass. I have purposed* **it;** *I will also do it." Isaiah 46:9-11 (NKJV)*

"For I know the thoughts I think toward you, says the Lord, thoughts of peace and not of evil, to give you a future and a hope." Jeremiah 29:11 (NKJV).

3. The word of God grows us personally.

God's word is the spiritual food that strengthens us from within. Dwelling on the word of God gives us the strength we need daily to go on.

Your words were found, and I ate them, and your words became to me a joy and the delight of my heart, for I am called by your name, O LORD, God of hosts. Jeremiah 15:16 (ESV)

My fellow believers, when it appears you are facing nothing, but difficulties see it as an invaluable opportunity to experience the greatest joy you can! For you know that when your faith is tested, it stirs up power within you to endure all things. And then as your endurance grows even stronger, it will release perfection into every part of your being until there is nothing missing and nothing lacking. ***James 1:2-4 (TPH)***

4. The word of God gives us God's viewpoint.

Nothing that happens to you is an accident. By studying how He used adversity in the lives of biblical characters, we get to understand how He may want to use our present struggles. God hasn't changed, and He is working something greater in our lives, just like a tapestry or a painting. The artist knows that the dark strokes will bring the painting to life; it is part of the process that will create a beautiful masterpiece in the end.

But let patience have its perfect work, that you may be perfect and complete, lacking nothing. James 1:4 (NKJV)

Dear friends, now we are children of God, and what we will be has not yet been made known. But we know that when Christ appears, we shall be like him, for we shall see him as he is. 1 John 3:2 (NIV)

Just as a ship's anchor is of no use unless it is lowered to the bottom, the Word of God cannot encourage us unless we take the time to study it and meditate on it. Pondering on the Lord's promises and how He proved His faithfulness to believers in the past encourages us to trust for what He will do in our lives. You must also believe what it says and do not doubt God's promises. As you apply it to your life, you will begin to see the manifestation of His words that never fail.

Chapter 6

The Purpose of Pain

I have a little confession to make. I struggled to write this chapter for a while and for several reasons. One of the reasons for this struggle was the fear of upsetting some readers who might still be in the initial stages of grief as they may not have gotten to the place of acceptance. This chapter looks deeply into why we are allowed to experience the level of loss and pain that we might be exposed to during our lifetime, and anyone who goes through pain will initially see no reason why they must go through such a thing. I want to make it known that this chapter is not to excuse what you are going through or brush it aside by attaching a reason to it. This chapter seeks to deliver the truth to us so that we can walk on the journey of grief with the bigger picture in mind and hope for what lies ahead.

The bible says that "ALL THINGS", not some things, work together for the good of them who love God and are called unto his purpose.[14] So even the loss and the pain are all working together for our good even though it might not look like it at this moment. You are shattered, you are struggling, you are crushed, and everything around you has fallen apart . . . but God. The unchanging God who made that promise cannot lie, and soon you will find out how true His word is.

After all, I had been through; I began to recognise pain for what it really is:

Pain is an agent of change.

Pain is the tearing down that allows for expansion. Pain is the renovation of the old, and when pain is allowed to complete its work, the new is born. I look at my life at this point and see the transformation that was done whilst I journeyed through my period of grief. I do not mean to say that losing my child was a good thing, but in the midst of my loss, which was excruciatingly painful, God worked something good.

As we know, God is not the source of pain and loss, even though He allows it. When we focus on our pain, the devil comes with his lies to make us believe that God sent it to us, but the truth is that the source of all pain and evil is the devil himself. We see it clearly in the case of job. The Person who inflicted all the pain Job experienced was the devil, though God allowed him, proving to the devil that He has the ultimate power when the devil couldn't take job's life. Job's pain took him on a journey of discovery of who God really is, coming out stronger and wiser than he was before.

I will take us through a number of analogies that will explain the purpose of pain.

Analogy 1: Silver and The Silversmith

A woman went to a silversmith to watch the process of refining silver. As she watched the silversmith, he held a piece of silver over the fire and let it heat up. He explained that in refining silver, one needed to hold the silver in the middle of the fire where the flames were hottest to burn away all the impurities.

The woman thought about God holding us in such a hot spot, and her mind was drawn to Malachi 3:3 (NKJV): "He sits as a refiner and purifier of silver." She asked the silversmith if it was true that he had to sit there in front of the fire the whole time as the silver was being refined. The man answered in the affirmative. Not only did he have to sit there holding the silver, but he also had to keep his eyes on the silver the entire time it was in the fire. If the silver was left a moment too long in the flames, it would be destroyed. The woman stood silent for a moment. Then she asked the silversmith how he would know when the silver is fully refined. He smiled at her and answered:

"That's easy. When I see my image in it." [15]

I find this very profound. From the bible, we learn that God is the Refiner, and He uses the heat of life to purify us into a pure picture of Himself.[16] This analogy reflects just that. As the heat applied to silver is for the purpose of purification, so is the heat we go through in life for a specific purpose.

Analogy 2: The Vine and the Vinedresser

A vinedresser went out to his vineyard to inspect his harvest. Walking through the clusters, he realised that some of the branches had overgrown and were not producing the harvest he expected to see. Wielding his pruning shear, he began to snip carefully at the branches that needed pruning. He walked through the entire vineyard and snipped away until he was satisfied. In time, he produced a bountiful harvest because he had taken the time to prune his vine.

Isn't that like what we experience when we go through loss? Isn't It's like something has been cut away from us? For the vine to be fruitful, there must be pruning, and irrespective of the pain at that moment, when the time of harvest arrives, the vines produce much more than it would have if it weren't pruned. There is pain in the cutting away we experience, but afterwards, we experience a greater level of fruitfulness.

"I am the true vine, and my father is the vinedresser. Every branch in me that does not bear fruit he takes away, and every branch that does bear fruit he prunes, that it may bear more fruit. John 15: 1-2 (NKJV)"

Analogy 3: The Clay and The Potter

A group of children went on a trip to a potter's house. On arrival, they saw a heap of clay in the corner but lined up on the other end of the room were beautifully finished pottery. None of them could imagine how what was once a heap of clay transformed into bespoke pieces of art, but they were there to find out just that. As they watched on, the Potter took a piece of clay from the heap and began beating and kneading it till it was soft enough to be placed on the wheel. Applying a generous amount of water to the clay, the Potter pushed the clay to the Centre of the spinning wheel and with the force of his hands, kept it spinning in the Centre. The kids watched on with careful anticipation of what would happen next. Pressing his fingers into the Centre of the clay, the Potter created a hole in the middle, and it took shape as he moved his hands back and forth creating the wall of the vessel, moulding it into shape. Satisfied with what he created; the Potter set the clay aside to dry. Confused, one of the children asked why he had abandoned the one he just shaped. The Potter responded by saying that if he placed the wet one in the oven, it would be destroyed from the heat. The Potter opened the oven and reached for a dry pot and began to glaze it to make it waterproof. Once he was done, he set it back in another oven. The children were shocked. It had just come from one oven and was going back to another. But that was the process, the Potter explained. The pot would remain in the oven for a much longer time until it was ready to be used.

Does this sound familiar? Isn't this how our life trials present themselves? Long spells of battering and intense heat? A time of rest and then some more heat that lasts even much longer? There is nothing pleasant about being in the fire of preparation, but as the clay, the heat is important to make us whole and complete, making us stronger and more refined. *See Psalm 66:10 of the Holy Bible.*

For us to be useful, we must first be wedged and centred and pulled and trimmed and handled and dried and fired and glazed and fired again. The pathway to purpose is painful, but the traumatic experiences are merely routes to glory. We are more inclined to pull away from the blades of the pruning shears, but you don't get to choose what gets pruned in your life. Birth pangs and the pain associated with pushing are all necessary for the birthing process. Grapes must be crushed in other to get wine. Olives or nuts must be crushed to bring forth oil. The purpose of pain is to birth purpose. It births productivity. The crushing brings pain, but it leads to gain.

Within these three analogies, there is a common theme: the level of care and sensitivity to make sure that what these artisans are working on is not destroyed. This is the same with God. He doesn't allow you to go through more than you can bear. It feels unbearable, but you bear it still because He carries you through it all. As I write this, I hear God say:

"No matter what you are dealing with, I have got this, and I have got your back."

We often ask ourselves why bad things happen to good people. I did this when Anu passed away. Also, a year or so after I took in and was expecting another child but in the third month, I had a miscarriage. It all didn't make sense to me. I didn't think this was fair, and I honestly couldn't fathom the purpose of the pain. I remember asking "*God why me?*" and I heard a voice vividly say,

"Why not you?".

Why must pain be the path to achieving purpose? I can't claim to have the answers, but the simple truth is that pain is painful, but it produces much gain. All the trials we go through only come to make us stronger. Every tragedy, loss or difficulty you go through isn't meant to kill you but push you to total dependency on God. As Christians, the mere fact that you are a believer is enough reason for adversity. This is because the enemy wants to make sure you deny God. There are a treasure and purpose inside of you, and the enemy doesn't want it revealed.

It is important to note that your pain is not a sign of failure or shortcomings. It is more a sign of innate greatness. Even Jesus endured hardship and pain. He endured the cross before He received the crown. See Hebrews 5:8.

Nothing takes God by surprise. He is in control of every season, every process and every bit of our lives. And all He has in store for us is good. All He does is good. He has a track record of being good. I have learnt through this experience that in trouble, in pain and my dark seasons, there is always more than meets the eye. So, my question changed from *"why me"* to

"God, what are you preparing me for?"

I remember when I was pregnant and was told about the pain of labour. I experienced that pain in my first delivery. If I looked at that pain and decided I wouldn't go through it anymore, I would have stopped having children. The experience I gained the first time gave me the wisdom to know that the pain is only temporal, and when the baby comes, I will be surrounded with so much joy that the pain would be a thing of the past.

Glory, lifting and greatness is birth through suffering. After Suffering, Jesus received a crown and a matchless name. His suffering, won us our victory. The pain is there, and it is overwhelming, but it is important not to be mindful of the pain to the point that we lose sight of the reward that is to come.

The Bible in Psalm 30:5b says:

"Weeping may endure for a night, but joy comes in the morning. (NKJV)

We may weep through the night, but at daybreak, it will turn into shouts of ecstatic joy. (TPH)

Many times, I have tried to stay up through the night to pray, and there were times when it seemed like the night was crawling. But time is always ticking, and the dawn must break forth. So also, is it with the pain you feel in your heart? The emptiness and loneliness that results from the loss of a loved one will someday become a memory. We will never stop missing the ones we lost, but it will not hurt as much.

I had an interview on dealing with loss, and afterwards, a young lady shared with me her experience of losing her mum when she was young. She said she wanted to know if we ever forget them. The truth is that we will always remember them. Many things will bring them to our memories; their birthdays, smell of their perfume, favourite song or favourite meal. But the fact that we do not forget them doesn't mean that the pain will remain forever. So treasure the precious memories you shared, and know that you will be just fine.

A few years have passed since I lost my daughter. At first, I thought I would never smile again, and the pain would last forever. As I look back, there have been more days to celebrate and laugh than days to cry. I have learnt not to take my eyes off the fact that in all these, God has the master plan. In the beginning, I couldn't see all these, and I couldn't think or accept this either, but with time, in the fullness of time, things began to unfold.

God's Goodness in our Grieving

Oh, taste and see that the LORD is good; Blessed is the man who trusts in Him! Psalm 34:8(NKJV)

Open your mouth and taste, open your eyes, and see—how good GOD is. Blessed are you who run to him'. Psalm 34:8 (MSG)

For the LORD is good; His mercy is everlasting, And His truth endures to all generations Psalm 100:5 (NKJV)

For the Lord is always good. He is ready to receive you. He's so loving that it will amaze you—so kind that it will astound you! And he is famous for his faithfulness toward all. Everyone knows our God can be trusted, for he keeps his promises to every generation! Psalm 100:5 (MSG)

Through this journey, one thing I struggled with was the idea of the goodness of God. In my current state, I have concluded which I would like to share.

"God is good" is not a cliché; it is the TRUTH.

So many questions have arisen in the question of the goodness of God, and I believe you might have come across a number of them:

"Is God really good

"If you say God is good, why do bad things happen?

"If God is good, why a million of people dying from a virus?"

"If God is good, why did I lose my job?"

"If God is good, why did my child die?"

We associate 'goodness' to positive occurrences, so the reason we struggle with this character of God is that we associate His goodness to things that happen in our lives that make us feel good. But is this the right way? God's character is irrespective of us. He is who He is. He is good, not just because He causes things that seem or feel 'good' to happen in our lives, but because that is just who He is. Amid the storms, He comes closer to us than the storm could ever be. No matter how bad the storm is, no matter how much pain we experience, no matter how different the outcome is from what we've prayed for, He remains good. I also pondered on this in the most challenging moment of my life after losing my child, but by His grace, I chose to believe that God is good no matter what, and I trusted and kept watching for the next opportunity that would unveil His ultimate plan through the process.

I have concluded that life can be hard, but God is good. He doesn't just do good things, He is good. He is the embodiment of GOOD. It's not just what He does, its who He is. His goodness is beyond my comprehension, but it is not beyond my experience. I desire to abide in this experience consciously. God is authentically good, and His goodness will follow me all the days of my life.

God is just as good to the man whose cancer was discovered early enough to be treated, as he is to the Person who did not catch it early and died weeks after. He is just as good to the people who died in the car accident as He is to the people who avoided it. He is just as good to the parents of obedient children as He is to parents of children who have rebelled. He is just as good to the woman longing to carry her baby in her hands as He is to women who have as many biological children as they want.

He is just as good to the family who loses their home in a fire, flood, or due to bankruptcy as He is to the family whose house does not burn down. He is just as good to the single Person as He is to the person who gets married. God remains good even though some people lost their jobs in the corporate downsizing while some earned a promotion. He is just as good when the tsunami claimed lives while others were rescued. God's goodness is not dependent on an outcome or an emotion or a near-miss-encounter. His goodness is not rated based on our avoidance of danger. God is good because when the storms of life hit, He holds us in His loving arms.

Friends, being anchored in the goodness of God isn't the most rational thing, but a stubborn unrelenting determination not to let the hardship of life downsize the goodness of our God will carry us safely to full recovery.

"Could the worst moments of your life become turning points of triumph for God, the Master Vintner, as He uses your life's deepest heartaches and most devastating disappointments for your good and His glory? What if you could see your life as

God sees it? What if your best moments are waiting ahead? My friend, I'm convinced God can use the weight crushing your soul right now to create His choicest wine if you will let Him" - TD Jakes[17]

Conclusion

Almost everyone, adults and children alike, face distress when someone close dies. Yet the nature of the misery and its manifestation depend on a host of many factors. The nature of the death, the nature and meaning of the relationship, and perceptions about adequacy of social support before and after the death are some of the factors, and they greatly influence the outcomes of the grieving process.

For many, the healing that occurs through the exploration and recognition of grief does not begin until loss has arisen. But for some, there is a profound recognition of the work that is to be done to meet our pain and our suffering now; to finish our business and allow each moment to be new[18]. We see so clearly the necessity of breaking the continuum of old pain – of old separation and grief that has often limited our experience of life, or ourselves, and of each other. Meeting the grief in mind, meeting the grieving world with more wisdom and forgiveness, will enable you to enter the healing moment fully alive.

Making the decision to move forward births newness. We definitely become a new creature because of our grief. The word newness is used because no one should expect you to act the same way. From the feeling of being a victim, the warrior in you will arise because you have battled incredible forces and you have survived.

From this situation you will discover hidden strengths you did not realize you had. You now have a new normal, and how you will view reality has radically changed. You will find eventually that your priorities and even perspective to life will change.

Learning how to deal with loss in a godly way helps you realise these:

- The Holy Spirit, once allowed to work in you, can lead you to the most reasonable results.
- You need a power greater than you, and a greater source of joy to overcome adversity such as grief.
- Grief is a process that is perhaps there to teach us something
- The cross of Jesus is proof that you can overcome pain because He rose victoriously for us.

[1] Grief: From Wikipedia, the free encyclopedia & grief and loss - the effects of grief and how to deal with

[2] Moving Forward: Dealing With Grief - Focus on the Family.

[3] Living Through Grief: Spiritual Life on CBN.com.

[4] *Grief and faith: the relationship between belief and grief*

[5] Miller, William A. *When going to Pieces Holds You Together*. Minneapolis: Augsburg, 1976.

[6] It's okay to Grieve: A Biblical Look at Losing a Loved One.

[7] March 12, 2014, Don't tell me to Move on- Kays Blog, Grief and Faith: the relationship between belief and grief1

[8] Blessed Be the name of the Lord: Matt Redman

[9] 4 Things Christians Should Know about Grief.

[10] The Guardian March 2017 How to live & learn from great loss: Joanna Moorhead

[11] Finding Hope in the Darkness of Grief | FamilyLife.

[12] www.griefrecoverymethod.co.uk

[13] The Grief Recovery Method Guide for Loss

[14] Romans 8:28 KJV Bible

[15] Primal by Mark Batterson & The Story of the
Silversmith | Silent Word Ministries.

[16] The Refiner's Fire - a lesson from the process of refining

[17] Crushing: God Turns Pressure into Power by T. D. Jakes

...

[18] From "The Grief Process" - Conclusion By Stephen
Levine

Lightning Source UK Ltd.
Milton Keynes UK
UKHW020301240821
389338UK00008B/508